20 GREATES

- A Mighty Fortress Is Our God
- All Hail The Power Of Jesus' Name
- Amazing Grace
- Be Thou My Vision
- Blessed Assurance
- Come, Thou Fount of Every Blessing
- Come, Thou Long-Expected Jesus
- He Leadeth Me
- Holy, Holy, Holy
- How Great Thou Art
- It Is Well With My Soul
- Jesus Paid It All
- Jesus Loves Me
- Just As I Am
- Love Divine, All Loves Excelling
- My Hope Is Built On Nothing Less
- O For A Thousand Tongues To Sing
- Rock Of Ages
- To God Be The Glory
- What A Friend We Have In Jesus

ARRANGED BY B. C. DOCKERY

A Mighty Fortress Is Our God

Martin Luther

B. C. Dockery

Arr. ©2022

Vc.

Vc.

All Hail the Power of Jesus' Name

Oliver Holden

B. C. Dockery

Arr. ©2022

All Hail the Power of Jesus' Name

Amazing Grace

John Newton
B. C. Dockery

Be Thou My Vision

Traditional
B. C. Dockery

Arr. ©2022

Vc.

Vc.

Blessed Assurance

Phoebe P. Knapp
B. C. Dockery

Vc.

Vc.

Come, Thou Fount of Every Blessing

Traditional
B. C. Dockery

Cello

Vc.

Come, Thou Fount of Every Blessing

Come, Thou Long-Expected Jesus

Rowland H. Prichard

B. C. Dockery

He Leadeth Me

William B. Bradbury
B. C. Dockery

Arr. ©2022

Holy, Holy, Holy

John B. Dykes

Score

How Great Thou Art

Traditional
B. C. Dockery

Arr. ©2022

It Is Well with My Soul

Philip P. Bliss
B. C. Dockery

Cello

Vc.

Arr. ©2022

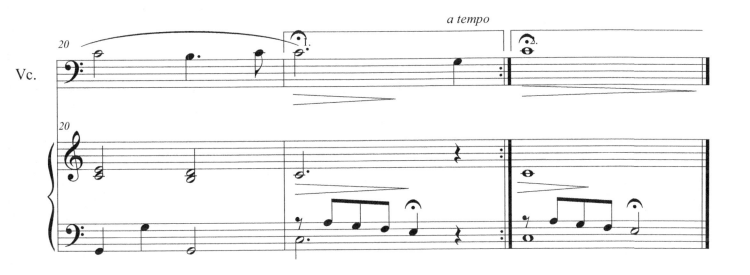

Jesus Paid It All

John T. Grape
arr. B. C. Dockery

Jesus Loves Me

William B. Bradbury
arr. B. C. Dockery

Just as I Am

William B. Bradbury
B. C. Dockery

Cello

Vc.

Arr. ©2022

Love Divine, All Loves Excelling

John Zundel
B. C. Dockery

Arr. ©2022

Vc.

Vc.

My Hope Is Built On Nothing Less

William B. Bradbury
B. C. Dockery

Arr. ©2022

Vc.

Vc.

O for a Thousand Tongues to Sing

Carl G. Glazer
B. C. Dockery

Arr. ©2022

Rock of Ages

Thomas Hastings

B. C. Dockery

To God Be the Glory

B. C. Dockery

What a Friend We Have in Jesus

Charles C. Converse
B. C. Dockery

Arr. ©2022

A Mighty Fortress Is Our God

Martin Luther

B. C. Dockery

Cello 1

Arr. ©2022

A Mighty Fortress Is Our God

Martin Luther
B. C. Dockery

Arr. ©2022

All Hail the Power of Jesus' Name

Oliver Holden

B. C. Dockery

Cello 1

Arr. ©2022

All Hail the Power of Jesus' Name

Oliver Holden
B. C. Dockery

Amazing Grace

John Newton
B. C. Dockery

Cello

Vc.

Vc.

Vc.

Amazing Grace

John Newton
B. C. Dockery

Be Thou My Vision

Traditional
B. C. Dockery

Cello 1

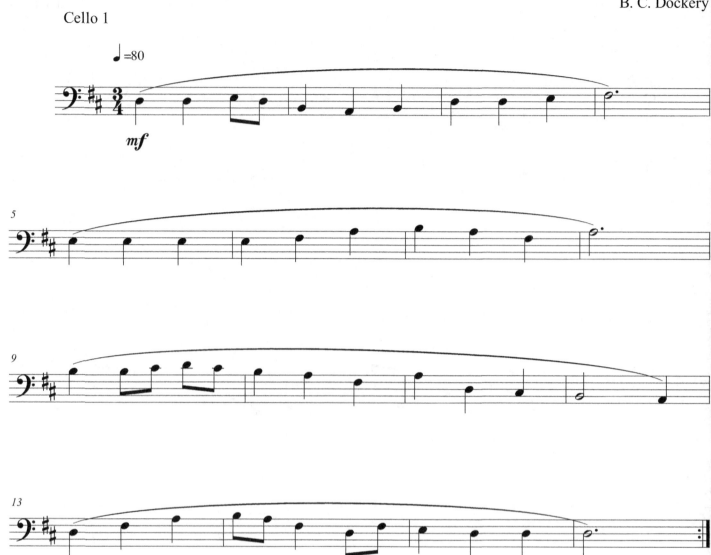

Be Thou My Vision

Traditional
B. C. Dockery

Piano

Arr. ©2022

Blessed Assurance

Phoebe P. Knapp

B. C. Dockery

Cello 1

Blessed Assurance

Phoebe P. Knapp
B. C. Dockery

Piano

Arr. ©2022

Come, Thou Fount of Every Blessing

Traditional
B. C. Dockery

Come, Thou Fount of Every Blessing

Traditional
B. C. Dockery

Piano

Come, Thou Long-Expected Jesus

Cello I

Rowland H. Prichard

B. C. Dockery

Arr. ©2022

Come, Thou Long-Expected Jesus

Rowland H. Prichard
B. C. Dockery

Piano

♩ = 110

Arr. ©2022

He Leadeth Me

William B. Bradbury

B. C. Dockery

Cello 1

Arr. ©2022

He Leadeth Me

William B. Bradbury

B. C. Dockery

Piano

Arr. ©2022

Cello I

Holy, Holy, Holy

John B. Dykes

Holy, Holy, Holy

John B. Dykes

Piano

How Great Thou Art

Cello I

Traditional
B. C. Dockery

How Great Thou Art

Traditional
B. C. Dockery

Piano

It Is Well with My Soul

Cello I

Philip P. Bliss
B. C. Dockery

It Is Well with My Soul

Piano

Philip P. Bliss
B. C. Dockery

It Is Well with My Soul

Cello I

Jesus Paid It All

John T. Grape
arr. B. C. Dockery

Jesus Paid It All

Piano

John T. Grape
arr. B. C. Dockery

Jesus Loves Me

Cello I

William B. Bradbury
arr. B. C. Dockery

Jesus Loves Me

William B. Bradbury
arr. B. C. Dockery

Piano

Just as I Am

Cello I

William B. Bradbury
B. C. Dockery

Just as I Am

William B. Bradbury

B. C. Dockery

Piano

Arr. ©2022

Love Divine, All Loves Excelling

Cello I

John Zundel
B. C. Dockery

Arr. ©2022

Love Divine, All Loves Excelling

Piano

John Zundel
B. C. Dockery

Arr. ©2022

My Hope Is Built On Nothing Less

Cello I

William B. Bradbury
B. C. Dockery

My Hope Is Built On Nothing Less

Piano

William B. Bradbury

B. C. Dockery

Arr. ©2022

O for a Thousand Tongues to Sing

Cello I

Carl G. Glazer
B. C. Dockery

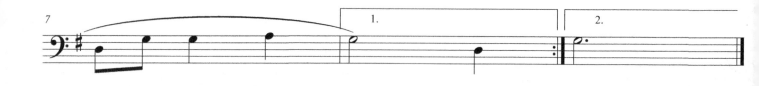

Arr. ©2022

O for a Thousand Tongues to Sing

Piano

Carl G. Glazer

B. C. Dockery

Rock of Ages

Cello I

Thomas Hastings
B. C. Dockery

Rock of Ages

Piano

Thomas Hastings
B. C. Dockery

Arr. ©2022

To God Be the Glory

Cello I

William H. Doane
B. C. Dockery

To God Be the Glory

Piano

William H. Doane
B. C. Dockery

What a Friend We Have in Jesus

Cello I

Charles C. Converse
B. C. Dockery

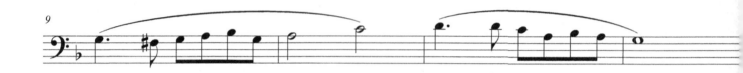

What a Friend We Have in Jesus

Piano

Charles C. Converse
B. C. Dockery

Made in the USA
Middletown, DE
25 September 2023

39338216R00051